Looking at Paintings

Self-portraits

The Painter and the Critic, date unknown
Pieter Brueghel, Flemish (1525/30—69)

LOOKING AT PAINTINGS

Self-portraits

Peggy Roalf

Series Editor
Jacques Lowe

Design
Joseph Guglietti and Steve Kalalian

Belitha Press
London

A
JACQUES LOWE
VISUAL ARTS PROJECTS
BOOK

Text © 1993 by Jacques Lowe Visual Arts Projects Inc.
A Jacques Lowe Visual Arts Projects Book

Printed in Italy

First published in the United States by Hyperion Books for Children

First published in the UK by
❧ Belitha Press Ltd
31 Newington Green, London N16 9PU

Cataloguing-in-publication data available from the British Library

ISBN 1 855 61 318 2

Original design concept by Amy Hill
UK editor: Kate Scarborough

Contents

In memory of my father, David Nathaniel Roalf

Introduction

*L*OOKING AT PAINTINGS is a series of books about the artistic process of seeing, thinking and painting. Painters have created self-portraits for many different reasons. For most artists, the face in the mirror is the most familiar and the most convenient model. They are working with a subject they know better than any other and are freer to experiment with new techniques.

Albrecht Dürer (page 9) portrayed himself as a thoughtful young scholar to show his future in-laws that he was the ideal husband for their beloved daughter. Rembrandt Harmenz van Rijn (page 15) displayed his genius for transforming paint into life in a youthful self-portrait, one of the first of the many Rembrandt painted throughout his career. Too poor to pay a model, Vincent van Gogh used himself in a series of portraits (page 25). He developed new ways of illustrating the changing effects of sunlight with brilliant colour and expressive brushstrokes.

Arshile Gorky's haunting self-portrait (page 37) expresses his love for his mother, who died when he was a teenager. Through the ghostly colours and church-like setting, he evokes his family's ancient religious beliefs. Using **primary colours**, Jacob Lawrence (page 43) created structural forms to represent himself as a builder of paintings. Audrey Flack (page 45) tricks the viewer into thinking that the painting is a photograph in a 1981 self-portrait.

Great artists' self-portraits reveal their character, and sometimes they reveal what the painters think about themselves. When you look into a mirror with the eyes of a painter, you begin to see the person behind the image.

Note: words in **bold** are explained in the glossary on pages 46-47.

PORTRAIT OF THE ARTIST HOLDING A THISTLE, 1493
Albrecht Dürer, German (1471–1528), parchment mounted on
canvas, 56 x 44 cm

*A*lbrecht Dürer had a long **apprenticeship** as a painter in his birthplace, Nuremberg, in Germany. Afterwards he continued to study painting during a four-year journey through Germany and Switzerland. While he was away from home, Dürer painted this self-portrait to show his future parents-in-law that he was an ideal husband for their beloved daughter.

The educated painter

By clothing himself in the robes of a scholar, Dürer reveals his belief that painters are learned people with a mission to educate. He holds a thistle, the traditional symbol of faithfulness, to show his devotion to both his art and his future wife. These features were intended to prove he was a worthy son-in-law.

In this portrait, Dürer used lines to shape the figure and to create a lively feeling of movement. Red bands outline the contours of his black silk robe and emphasize the shape of his shoulders and arms. He used lines softened by shading to suggest the fine linen which formed the many pleats of his tunic.

Lasting colours

Because of the technique Dürer used, the colours in the painting remain as clear today as they were five hundred years ago. Instead of canvas, he used an animal skin, called parchment, which was specially prepared for painting. Dürer gradually built up colours in thin layers called **glazes**. The **transparent** glazes allow the pale parchment to reflect light through the highlights that model his features and shape the folds of his cloak.

SELF-PORTRAIT, about 1514

Leonardo da Vinci, Italian (1452–1519), red chalk on paper, 32 x 21 cm

Leonardo da Vinci, the **Renaissance** master who painted the *Mona Lisa* and the *Last Supper*, was considered a genius by the people around him. Leonardo was not only a great painter and city planner, but also a scientist and an inventor. Among his five thousand or so pages of drawings are designs for complicated military fortifications and firearms, methods of draining swamps and a flying machine whose design is similar to the helicopter.

Lines and shading

This drawing, the only known self-portrait of the artist, was made during Leonardo's sixty-second year. He used finely sharpened red chalk called sanguine. With variations in line thickness, he created a realistic effect. Leonardo shaped the outline of the nose with a single line that changes from a thick stroke at the furrowed bridge to a very fine line that shows the bump in the middle. For shading Leonardo drew a series of parallel strokes called hatching. Leonardo's hatched lines slant from the upper left to the lower right, because he was left-handed.

Because Leonardo moved quickly from one idea to another, he had no time to organize his drawings, which cover an enormous range of subjects. Although many of these pages have been preserved in libraries and museums, many more were scattered and lost when the Frenchman Napoleon Bonaparte and his army invaded Italy in 1796.

Filippino Lippi created the soft shadows defining his features by applying light transparent colours, called glazes, over a painting made with darker tones.

11

PORTRAIT OF A YOUNG MAN, undated
Agnolo Bronzino, born Agnolo di Cosimo, Italian (1503–72)
oil on wood, 94 x 74 cm

Bronzino completed his artistic training in Florence, Italy, at a time when ideas about beauty in art were changing. The **classical** values of the Renaissance—ideal beauty, balance and harmony—were rejected in favour of a more emotional way of depicting people.

Focusing attention

In this painting, believed to be a self-portrait, Bronzino displays the artistic gifts that soon gained the attention of his greatest **patron**, Cosimo de' Medici, the Grand Duke of Tuscany. Bronzino created an strong presence with his casual, somewhat arrogant pose. The line made by the position of his shoulders and arms forms a triangle that fills the space between the table and chair. The background is purposefully off balance so that our eyes naturally return to the figure.

*Giuseppe Arcimboldo, who usually painted people as masses of delicate flowers, combined blue pencil and **ink** in this self-portrait.*

Cool colours

Bronzino's unusual **composition** is matched by his sophisticated use of colour. With cold shades of green and red, he created icy flesh tones softened only by the warm red in the lips. Bronzino added green to the black tunic and the white collar, giving the painting a cool feeling, which is emphasized by the magenta of the table. Both the colours and composition show the young man as a distant character.

Although Bronzino painted many **murals** for the Medici palace, he is remembered for his portraits of poets, philosophers and artists of his generation.

SELF-PORTRAIT, about 1629
Rembrandt Harmenz van Rijn, Dutch (1606–69), oil on panel, 37 x 29 cm

Rembrandt Harmenz van Rijn created more than eighty paintings of himself over a period of forty years. From the young man of twenty-three (opposite) to the older man in the drawing below, his self-portraits make up a revealing pictoral diary of an artist. The fact that Rembrandt painted so many self-portraits was unusual, because in the seventeenth century, self-portraits were considered a foolish subject compared with pictures of biblical and historical events.

In a drawing made in the 1650s, Rembrandt showed himself dressed for work. His stern expression suggests that he is examining a work in progress.

Power and mystery

Rembrandt projects an aura of power by wearing the armoured neck plate of a soldier. By balancing light and dark areas, a technique called chiaroscuro, he focuses attention on his eyes. Rembrandt almost masks one side of his face in reddish brown shadows, forming a contrast with the highlighted areas on the left side of the painting. This gives the painting a mysterious quality.

Mixing colours

Rembrandt rejected the usual methods of building up colours in thin layers that would give predictable results. Instead, he blended colours on the panel, creating variations in **tone** that make each brushstroke come to life. In this picture, Rembrandt added a golden colour to the skin, hair and bronze collar, which fills the portrait with warm light. With strokes of brilliant white paint on the lace collar, he made the deep shadows seem even darker.

THE ART OF PAINTING, about 1665
Jan Vermeer, Dutch (1632–75), oil on canvas, 118 x 98 cm

Jan Vermeer, who lived in the Netherlands during the seventeenth century, was better known in his lifetime as an art expert than as a painter. Today, the forty paintings that he produced are priceless.

A view inside the studio

Vermeer invites us into his studio to observe a work in progress. He is working on a painting of Clio, the ancient Greek **muse** of history. Vermeer gave this scene energy with his use of **perspective** and the ways in which he deliberately broke the rules. He conveys a sense of depth through the curtain framing the scene and the diagonal floor tiles that gradually become smaller towards the background. The model portraying Clio is in proportion to the furniture and room. However, the painter and the model are not in proportion to each other. If Vermeer had followed the rules of perspective exactly, the model would be too large for the room. Vermeer focuses attention on the artist by exaggerating his size and pose.

Vermeer achieved the bright light in this painting by restricting his **palette** to a few strong colours: ultramarine, vermilion and yellow. He painted Clio's dress in ultramarine, which he also used in the map, the fabric on the table and the tapestry. The red of the painter's stockings is deepened with brown to make the russet in the curtain and map. Vermeer covered the white wall and the artist's black jacket in the pale yellow of soft daylight, creating a feeling of warmth.

Hans Holbein the Younger created shadows with delicate parallel lines, called hatching, using chalk sharpened to a fine point.

SELF-PORTRAIT WITH TWO PUPILS, 1785
Adélaïde Labille-Guiard, French (1749–1803), oil, 207x 149 cm

*A*délaïde Labille-Guiard became a painter in France at a time when women were not allowed to study or teach in academic art schools. Labille-Guiard took private lessons and specialized in portraits. In 1782 she was close to being accepted by the influential French Academy. However, it was rumoured that her teacher, François André Vincent, completed her paintings. To disprove these claims, Labille-Guiard invited several prominent academicians to sit for portraits. They were impressed by her talent, and campaigned for her acceptance by the academy. She was finally elected in 1783. Labille-Guiard may have painted this self-portrait in 1785 as part of her struggle to create more opportunities for women artists.

In this detail we can see that Adélaïde Labille-Guiard, using fine brushstrokes, paid careful attention to every feather in her hat.

Spotlights

Labille-Guiard emphasized her presence by using dramatic contrasts between light and dark areas. Daylight pours in from the right to illuminate the artist, setting off her luxurious silken gown. She softened her hair, her skin and the shading in her dress with warm **umber** tones that, by contrast, emphasize the cool brilliant colours in the fabric.

Labille-Guiard gave this quiet scene a feeling of energy through the sweeping folds of her stylish gown. She painted the gown using a technique called fat over lean. Labille-Guiard first created the shaded areas with dark paint thinned with **turpentine**. After the thin, or lean, layer had dried, she applied gleaming highlights with paint thickened, or fattened, with oil.

19

MOTHER ANTONY'S TAVERN, 1866
Pierre-Auguste Renoir, French (1841–1919), oil on canvas, 191 x 127 cm

In the spring of 1866, Pierre-Auguste Renoir went out to the country with his former classmate Jules Le Coeur and another artist named Alfred Sisley. At night they often went to an inn called Mother Antony's, used by artists who came to paint in the nearby forest of Fontainebleau. Renoir created this self-portrait with his friends, Mother Antony and her dog, Toto, as a reminder of the good times and the discussions about painting they enjoyed.

A triangular composition

Renoir created a serious atmosphere by using dark colours, and by painting the attentive expressions of himself, standing, and Sisley, seated, listening to Le Coeur, in the straw hat. The figures are arranged in a triangular composition, with Renoir's head forming the **apex**. The design is emphasized by the ceiling beam on the right.

By staging this scene in sombre black, white and brown, Renoir focuses attention on the portraits. He created life-like flesh tones in their faces and hands by building up paint in transparent layers called glazes (see page 8). He formed the shadows defining Sisley's head with a blue-grey tone. Over this he added very thin see-through layers of ivory and pink that allow the bluish shadows to show through. This created soft, three-dimensional contours. He then applied white highlights on the forehead, nose and chin.

Gustave Courbet portrayed feelings of fear and desperation in this self-portrait drawn in the 1840s.

21

SELF-PORTRAIT IN A FLOWERED HAT, 1883

James Ensor, Belgian (1860–1949), oil on canvas, 76 x 53 cm

James Ensor grew up in the coastal city of Ostend, Belgium, where his parents owned a souvenir shop. Ensor was a daydreamer who hated school. His understanding parents allowed him to leave at the age of fifteen and study art in Brussels. The paintings he created—pictures of real life that were sometimes ugly—shocked and angered his teachers, who preferred beauty to realism.

The model artist

Ensor often used his own image to study expressions, gestures and emotions. He appears, thinly disguised, as a character in many of his major paintings. In this 1883 self-portrait, Ensor expressed the feeling that life is a series of tragic circumstances that are often disguised as comic events. Beneath a whimsical straw hat decorated with flowers and feathers, Ensor's face reveals his deep sadness.

Old style, new technique

The painter creates a solemn mood with dark colours and a vague background. As a tribute to the great Flemish painter Peter Paul Rubens (1577-1640), Ensor adopted the old master's style for his hair, beard and clothes. But he used a modern painting technique to show the play of light on his sharp features, applying bold thick strokes of paint. Ensor moulded the shape of his nose with a red shadow that suggests light reflected from the reddish background. In contrast to the expressive details that form the face and hat, the jacket is a simple triangle of black.

SELF-PORTRAIT WITH STRAW HAT, about 1888
Vincent van Gogh, Dutch (1853–90), oil on canvas, 40 x 31 cm

In 1886, Vincent van Gogh moved to Paris, France, to live with his brother Theo. Because he was too poor to hire models, van Gogh painted self-portraits in which he experimented with new ideas. In this portrait, van Gogh's **signature style** emerged in an explosion of brushstrokes.

Van Gogh shaped his straw hat, face and jacket with directional strokes of paint. He formed the hat with curved parallel lines of yellow, tan and green that define its contours and texture. Diagonal marks define the sharp planes of his cheeks and forehead. Van Gogh's intense expression combined with vigorous dashes of thick paint create a feeling of restless energy.

In this 1896 painting made in Tahiti, Paul Gauguin expressed the despair he felt when poor health and poverty prevented him from returning to Europe to visit his

Brilliant shadows

The wonder of this painting is the way in which van Gogh created the effect of transparent shadows with brilliant rather than dark colours. Van Gogh applied bright colours side by side over a tan background, which he left partly uncovered between brushstrokes. Instead of mixing paint on a palette, van Gogh applied strokes of red and green that merge in the viewer's eyes with the muted tan to create a shadow on the forehead. Dashes of chrome yellow on the face, neck and jacket become reflections of the yellow hat. The triangle of white forming his shirt emphasizes the clear, bright tone of the portrait.

SELF-PORTRAIT WITH A PALETTE, 1906
Pablo Picasso, Spanish (1881–1973), oil on canvas, 90 x 72 cm

In the spring of 1906, Pablo Picasso visited the remote mountain village of Gósol, Spain. Here he was fascinated by a simply carved wooden sculpture dating from the twelfth century. Picasso shaped a small statue from a gnarled stick, using the natural curves of the wood to shape the figure.

A carved image

The process of carving inspired Picasso to change the way he painted people. In this mask-like self-portrait, he stripped away distracting details in the same way he had removed unnecessary wood to sculpt the little statue. He painted only the lines and shapes that clearly conveyed the forms of his head and body.

Blocks of colour

Picasso used his brush like a chisel, painting with a range of colours that can be seen in Gósol's rocky terrain: umber, **sienna**, grey and white. He defined the eyes, jaw and hairline with oval shapes and used a triangle for the nose. Patches of white and black emphasize the sharp angles of the face. He painted the figure with blocks of colour, using umber lines that vary in thickness to convey the solid form. The torso is a flatly painted square of white broken by grey brushstrokes that create a sense of bulk. With bold, rounded lines, he emphasized his broad chest and powerful right arm. Picasso scrubbed a thin layer of white paint over umber for the background.

SELF-PORTRAIT, 1912
Otto Dix, German (1891–1968), oil and tempera on panel, 72 x 48 cm

Otto Dix grew up in the working-class town of Unternhaus, Germany. Encouraged by a teacher who recognized Dix's unusual gift for drawing, he left school to study art at the age of fourteen. Dix first worked for a decorative artist, learning the techniques of painting. He then enrolled in the Dresden School of Arts and Crafts. In the Dresden museums, he studied the work of Albrecht Dürer, who is regarded as a hero in Germany. Dix created this self-portrait in order to study painting techniques perfected four hundred years earlier by Renaissance artists.

Influences

Dix based this painting on Dürer's youthful self-portrait (page 9). The pose is nearly identical, down to the flower held between his thumb and forefinger. But Dix, who was also moved by Vincent van Gogh's emotional self-portraits, created an uneasy feeling through the scowling expression and the harsh lighting.

Like sixteenth-century German artists, Dix used a wooden panel, which lasts longer than canvas. Dix created skin tones and the texture of corduroy by applying glazes (see page 8). Drawing with fine brushes and dark brown paint, he created contrasting tones in the jacket and hair. In this picture, Dix mastered an old technique. The craft of painting was important to Dix, who wanted his work to last.

Oscar Kokoshka, a contemporary of Otto Dix, applied paint with thick brushstrokes called **impasto** *in this picture of himself at the* **easel**.

DOUBLE PORTRAIT WITH WINE GLASS, 1917
Marc Chagall, Russian (1887–1985), oil on canvas, 229 x 134 cm

When he was a student in Russia, Marc Chagall's teachers laughed at his imaginative way of painting. They thought he lacked the skill to paint the world the way it appeared to them. In 1910, Chagall moved to Paris, France, where he was free to work in his own style. His paintings show a fantasy world in which people, animals and objects drifted through dream-like landscapes. They captivated the people who saw his first exhibition in 1914. Chagall joyously returned to Russia. There, however, he was still unknown. Chagall painted this lyrical wedding portrait of himself and his wife, Bella, who supported him with love and companionship while he struggled once again to establish his reputation.

Shapes and colour

Chagall **stylized** the figures. They divide the canvas into two areas of contrasting colours: a cool misty white on the left and a fiery golden blaze on the right. Using a narrow range of **complementary** colours— red and green, purple and yellow—he emphasized the figures against the brown tones in the distant city.

Chagall's bright colours and joyful smile make us feel the happiness he and his wife, Bella, felt on their wedding day.

Chagall made this painting gleam like a stained glass window. He painted the faces smoothly in ivory and brown, modelling the features with soft shading and highlights. He shaped his jacket as a flat red **silhouette.** He formed the mottled background on the right by applying yellow and orange over a greenish background. This shows through as the shapes of the clouds.

30

WHERE FRIENDS MEET, 1922
Max Ernst, German (1891–1976), oil on canvas, 127 x 191 cm

Max Ernst was horrified by the destructiveness of the First World War, the first war to use aeroplanes. He joined a group of artists who formed a new approach to painting, sculpture, poetry and the theatre called **surrealism.** They rejected rational thinking in favour of dreams, which they believed was the only true reality.

Is it a dream?

Ernst painted this imaginary group portrait of the leading surrealists and their heroes, including Sigmund Freud, the first **psychiatrist** to interpret dreams. Ernst portrayed himself as the seated man wearing a green suit (4). He created a dream-like quality by combining realistic and unbelievable elements. The faces are as life-like, but some are black and white, like the photographs of the time, and some are painted in colour. The figures are seated but do not have chairs. And they are all gathered on an frozen waste rather than in a room.

Ernst created an uneasy atmosphere by distorting the perspective. The large figures of poets Paul Eluard (9) and André Breton (13) loom over the people sitting in the foreground. The Russian author Fyodor Dostoyevski (6) is much bigger than the others in the front row. The apple held by sculptor Jean Arp (5) is bigger than the one in the foreground. None of it makes sense.

This detail shows the artist in a suit and tie, as are all the other subjects. This makes their location seem even stranger.

SELF-PORTRAIT IN TUXEDO, 1927
Max Beckmann, German (1884–1950), oil on canvas, 139 x 94 cm

When the First World War broke out in 1914, Max Beckmann said to his wife Minna, 'I will not shoot at the French. I've learned too much from them'. As an army ambulance driver, however, Beckmann witnessed death and destruction at the front lines. The experience was so disturbing that he suffered a nervous breakdown in 1915. After recovering, Beckmann returned to a Germany destroyed by foreign occupation, economic depression and hunger. Here he searched for his identity an artist in a series of powerful self-portraits.

By 1927, when he painted this image, Beckmann had achieved public acclaim. Wearing elegant evening clothes, he strikes an aristocratic pose that projects a sense of power and pride.

During a visit to the Rocky Mountains in 1949, Beckmann portrayed himself as a fisherman. Sharp, rounded lines and expressive shading emphasize his powerful hands grasping a rope.

Strong image

Beckmann painted this portrait in harsh lighting using only black, white and brown paint. He divided the figure down the middle, putting the left side in deep shadow and illuminating the right side with glaring light. He defined the strong features on the right with brilliant, poster-like highlights that create a bold effect in contrast to the flatly painted figure. Beckmann made the black suit seem even blacker with a blaze of white that forms the shirt. The ghostly background, painted in broad patches of silver grey, emphasizes the dynamic outline of the figure.

THE ARTIST AND HIS MOTHER, about 1926–34
Arshile Gorky, American, (1905–48), oil on canvas, 150 x 125 cm

*A*rshile Gorky was born in Armenia with the surname Adoian. His happy childhood ended abruptly in 1915, when Turkish forces invaded Armenia and seized the Adoian's farm. His family fled to a remote mountain village to escape persecution, but four years later Gorky's mother died of starvation. At the age of fifteen, Gorky travelled alone to the United States to join two sisters who had left Armenia two years earlier.

A religious influence

Gorky developed an appreciation of icons—paintings used in religious ceremonies—from his mother, who was descended from generations of **Eastern Orthodox** priests. In this self-portrait, Gorky depicts himself as a child offering flowers to his beloved mother, posed to resemble an icon of the Virgin Mary.

Gorky makes us feel that we are in another time because of the almost church-like setting, the figures that seem to float in space and the pale colours. He simplified the figures with flatly painted areas of white, muted yellow and grey, and created a sense of mass through the curves of the silhouetted forms. The expressive brush marks on the clothes, in contrast to the crisp outlines, give a feeling of movement to this otherwise still scene.

Gorky gave the faces distinctive shapes and shadows. He painted the roundness of his head with arcs forming the hairline. Gorky painted his mother's face as an oval, which he rounded with simple shading that defines her features and the shadow cast by her veil.

SELF-PORTRAIT WITH A BEER STEIN, about 1935
Philip Evergood, American (1901–73), mixed media, 40 x 30 cm

Philip Evergood was a rebel. His wealthy family sent him to Cambridge University in England to study law, but he left to study painting and sculpture. When he returned to New York City, Evergood took a job as a handyman and continued to paint during his time off. He depicted the misery caused by the Great Depression of the 1930s in paintings that showed the terrible problems of the poor and unemployed. Evergood also believed in the power of art to create happiness.

A lively style

In this painting, Evergood invites us to join a party. His portrait is shaped with bold black lines that define his features and hands as clearly as in a comic strip. With a palette knife, a tool used for blending paint, he applied the colours thickly and added more paint with a brush, stirring up textures to form the curves of his cheeks and jaw.

The background party

In contrast to the clear lines and direct style of the self-portrait, Evergood painted the partygoers with bold brushwork and primary colours. He created the shadowy effect of a dark nightclub by laying a film of transparent black paint over the background. Streaks of bright yellow next to the lamps focus attention on the women's dresses.

Philip Evergood used a soft, sharp pencil to create velvety shading on rough textured paper, making the white areas in this drawing gleam with light.

SELF-PORTRAIT WITH MONKEY, 1938
Frida Kahlo, Mexican (1907–54), oil, 40 x 30 cm

Frida Kahlo was one of the first generation of women to be offered a free education in Mexico. Her life and art were influenced by this new freedom for Mexican women and by personal tragedy. Kahlo studied native Mexican painting and folklore, which she later incorporated into her art.

In this self-portrait, Kahlo projects awareness of her powers as an artist and her pride as a woman. She constructs a sharply detailed and richly coloured image. Using fine brushes, Kahlo created textures in the prickly cactus and jagged leaves in the background, forming a striking contrast to her smooth skin.

Balance

Kahlo balanced the composition with vertical and rounded forms. She emphasized her long neck with the lines of the tall cactus on the right. The roundness of her eyes and the monkey's is echoed by the **pre-Columbian** necklace and her rounded neckline. Kahlo gave the picture depth by painting a blue area that suggests a distant sky and the cool greens that seem to fade backwards. In contrast, her head and shoulders, painted in warm tones, loom above the jungle. With a glimpse of humour, Kahlo copied her expression in the monkey's face.

In the background of this 1944 self-portrait, the Mexican painter Diego Rivera included a section of his mural showing a flower vendor.

40

41

THE STUDIO, 1977
Jacob Lawrence, American (born 1917), gouache, 75 x 55 cm

Jacob Lawrence grew up in New York City during the Harlem Renaissance of the 1930s. He was influenced by African-American poets and philosophers, who urged young artists to discover their heritage.

The contemporary artist Paul Cadmus remembered his youth in this dual self-portrait done with soft pencil on textured paper.

A high view point

In 1977, Lawrence painted *The Studio*, a self-portrait in which the artist's working space symbolizes his character. Lawrence constructed a scene bristling with the energy of bright primary colours. A zigzag stair rail slices through the room. He chose a high point of view and tilted the floor down to show the viewer more of the busy workplace. Lawrence exaggerated the size of his hands holding the tools of his trade to represent the artist's power as an image builder.

Gouache

Lawrence painted blocks of colour with **opaque** water-colour called **gouache**. He created a feeling of depth using variations of flat colour rather than shading and highlights. For example, he made the bright yellow wall seem distant with the patches of tan, which are formed by mixing yellow and brown and by painting the slanting white lines on the ceiling. Lawrence placed slabs of white around the stairs to make the figure stand out from the object-filled scene.

WE ARE ALL LIGHT AND ENERGY, 1981
Audrey Flack, American (born 1931), acrylic and oil, 115 x 165 cm

As a child, Audrey Flack preferred drawing and painting to studying academic subjects. With her father's encouragement, Flack began her formal training at New York City's High School of Music and Art, a public school for gifted young artists and musicians.

In the 1960s, Flack examined the different ways that light gives objects their colour and form. She observed that under extremely bright artificial light, ordinary objects were magically transformed. They seemed larger, more colourful and even more three-dimensional than they actually were.

A photograph or painting?

Flack's self-portrait with her parrot Alfred makes us think about the line separating reality and illusion. The painting, which is about four times larger than life size, has amazing clarity because of the intense colours she has used. The illusion is shattered only when we notice the bare canvas beneath the shadow of her necklaces and realize that this is a painting, not a photograph.

Flack created gradually changing levels of colour using a mechanical artists' tool called an **airbrush**. For the face, she applied lighter and darker tones over a medium skin colour to shape the curves. Because an airbrush breaks paint into tiny particles, the colours underneath gleam through to create the effect of light shining from within. The vague background, thickly painted with palette knives and brushes, emphasizes the sharp details in the portrait.

New York-based artist Cheryl Laemmle formed her features with vegetables and weeds in this humorous painting.

44

Glossary and Index

AIRBRUSH: a specially designed kind of pen that releases paint in very fine droplets.

APEX: the highest point.

APPRENTICESHIP: the training of a pupil by a master craftsman.

CANVAS: a woven fabric (often linen or cotton) used as a painting surface. It is usually stretched tight and stapled on to a wooden frame in order to produce a flat surface.

CLASSICAL: a term that refers to paintings and sculpture created by artists who admire and adopt the art of ancient Greece and Rome

COMPLEMENTARY: colours that fit together to make a whole picture. They suit each other.

COMPOSITION: the arrangement of objects and figures and the combination of colours and shapes.

EASEL: a frame for supporting a picture while it is being painted.

EASTERN ORTHODOX: the Greek Christian religion.

GLAZES: layers of partly **transparent** colour that give a glassy finish to a painting.

GOUACHE: an opaque form of **water-colour**, which is also called tempera or body colour.

IMPASTO: a method of painting using very thick layers of paint which keep the mark of the brush when they dry. You can apply this paint with anything you like, for example, a knife or your fingers.

INK: usually, a jet black fluid made of powdered carbon mixed with a water-soluble liquid. Ink drawings can be made with dark lines and diluted tones of grey. Inks are also made in colours.

MURAL: a very large painting that decorates a wall or is created as part of a wall. Also called a wall painting.

MUSE: a divine spirit who inspires artists.

OIL PAINT: **pigment** is combined with oil (usually linseed or poppy oil). Oil paint is never mixed with water. It is washed off brushes or thinned with **turpentine**. Oils dry slowly, allowing the artist to work on a painting for a long time.

OPAQUE: not letting light pass through. Opaque paints conceal what is under them. (The opposite of **transparent**.)

PALETTE: (1) a flat tray used by a painter for laying out and mixing colours. (2) The range of colours selected by a painter for a work.

PATRON: an individual or organization that supports the arts or an individual artist.

PERSPECTIVE: perspective is a method of representing people, places, and things in a painting or drawing to make them appear solid or three-dimensional rather than flat.

PIGMENT: the raw material that gives paint its colour. It can be made from natural or man-made minerals.

PRE-COLUMBIAN: something that is from the time before Columbus discovered South and Central America.

PRIMARY COLOURS: those colours from which all other colours can be obtained. They are red, orange, blue, yellow, green, indigo and violet.

PSYCHIATRIST: someone who is medically trained to treat diseases of the brain.

RENAISSANCE: a period of European history from the early 14th to the late 16th century. The name means 'rebirth' in French and marks the change from the Middle Ages to the Modern Age. The rebirth refers to the revival of arts, literature, politics, trade, science and medicine.

SIENNA: a fine **pigment** that is used in paint to make the colour reddish-brown.

SIGNATURE STYLE: the particular style of an artist which shows that the painting could only be done by that person.

SILHOUETTE: an image, such as a portrait or an object, that consists of the outline of its shape in a solid colour.

STYLIZED: to make a picture in a particular manner that is typical of the painter.

SURREALISM: a movement in French art, which started around 1920, that aimed at drawing from the subconscious and escaping the control of reason.

TEXTURE: the surface quality of a painting. For example, an oil painting could have a thin, smooth surface texture, or a thick, rough surface texture.

TONE: the colours used overall in a painting. For example, an artist might begin by painting the entire picture in shades of greenish grey. After more colours are applied using **transparent glazes**, shadows and highlights, the mass of greenish grey colour underneath will show through and create an even tone.

TRANSPARENT: allowing light to pass through so colours underneath can be seen. (The opposite of **opaque**.)

TURPENTINE: a strong-smelling solvent made from pine sap, used in oil painting.

UMBER: a pigment that is added to paint to creat the colour brown.

WATER-COLOUR: pigment is combined with a water-based substance. Water-colour paint is thinned with water, and areas of paper are often left uncovered to produce highlights. Water-colour paint was first used 37,000 years ago by cave dwellers who created the first wall paintings.

Credits